More Praise for
The ABCs of Full Tilt Living

* * *

"*The ABCs of Full Tilt Living* is an amazingly clear, concise, and effective set of antidotes to the problems and confusion that plague us in our lives. Maureen Smith offers us simple yet effective ways to embrace our lives with joy, achieve greater serenity despite the chaos that surrounds us, and cut through those challenges we find disturbing and disorienting. This is a book well worth reading, recommending, and keeping close at hand."

-CHARLES A. GARFIELD, Ph.D.,
author of *Peak Performers* and *Second to None*

* * *

"*The ABCs of Full Tilt Living* steps lightly from Ahhhhh to the Zone of peace and clarity where the best self is at home. It dares readers of all ages to have fun in life by creating the thoughts and actions that attract joyful, spontaneous moments on the wheel of happiness."

-LAUNA HUFFINES, author of
Healing Yourself With Light: How to Connect With the Angelic Healers and *Bridge of Light: Tools of Light for Spiritual Transformation*

(continued on next page)

"Browsing through these chock-full chapters felt like looking through an assortment of luscious teas . . . hmmm . . . Could I use a little zing? Or maybe some spice? Ooooh . . . minty . . . that's it! There's something here for everyone, for every occasion, for every mood. Enjoy!"

-BJ GALLAGHER, author of *Everything I Need to Know I Learned from Other Women*

• • •

"*The ABCs of Full Tilt Living* gives your life a little jump start just when you need it most. The whole book seems to crackle with energy; Maureen Smith's wise words bounce off the page and climb into that suffering little corner of your psyche that most needs cheering up. A marvelous antidote to a grim, workaday world."

-SUZANNE FALTER-BARNS, author of *How Much Joy Can You Stand?* and *Living Your Joy*

The ABCs
of Full Tilt Living

Insights from A–Z

Maureen Smith

To donna~
With wishes for
many "Full tilt" moments~
Maureen Smith

Red Wheel
Boston, MA / York Beach, ME

First published in 2003 by
Red Wheel/Weiser, LLC
York Beach, ME

With offices at:
368 Congress Street
Boston, MA 02210
www.redwheelweiser.com

Library of Congress Cataloging-in-Publication Data
Smith, Maureen (Maureen J.),
   The ABCs of full tilt living : insights from A-Z / Maureen
Smith.
       p. cm.
   ISBN 1-59003-048-6
   1. Conduct of life. I. Title.
   BF637.C5S5449 2003
   158.1--dc21

                                    2003010536

Typeset in AGaramond by Jill Feron/Feron Design
Printed in Canada
TCP

10 09 08 07 06 05 04 03
 8 7 6 5 4 3 2 1

Table of Contents

Turn
ordinary days
into Ahhs

Introduction
Insights from A-Z

My hope is that the thoughts hanging behind these twenty-six letters open the possibility for your life to go at *full tilt*. Throttle open, wind whipping, sky's the limit, no stopping you now!

The idea of A to Z isn't really mine. My inventive and enthusiastic publisher thought it might be fun to have an alphabet soup kind of approach to insights for full tilt living. Well, why not? So I dove in. What came out is bite-sized and just as disordered as alphabet soup. It's twenty-six invitations to take good care of yourself, let go of the stuff you don't need, open doorways to having more of what you want.

Turn ordinary days into Ahhs. Live out a secret wish to be a drama queen. Get help with the times when you want to kick yourself or feel flat as a pancake. Chase down that "zone" thing. Take some time out to get fresh, grounded.

Feel free to pick out the letters in whatever order they speak to you. And by all means, if any of these ideas have you doing that finger-in-the-mouth gagging thing, skip them. Stick with the ones that help you get past the speed bumps and other such diversions that might break your stride and take you away from finding the delight in your life. So that life for you can be full tilt.

Know that I'm behind you all the way.

Ahh!

Or more to the point, Aaaaahhhh!

Not to be confused with (A), as in the correct answer, the first item to be addressed, the main but not the only reason, the opening instruction, the necessary grade.

Lifting ourselves out of the hunt for the answer, the list of problems waiting to be solved, the need to explain, to instruct, to score.

Aaaaahhhh!

The sun is so warm.

The coffee's just right.

Who could have imagined a color so rich?

This is the most perfect _____ (pen, pair of pliers, desktop, potato peeler)!

Take some Aaaaahhhs into your world today. Be astonished, delighted, undone. Let your grip on your hard-edged, sharp-witted self go slack for a few seconds and ride the waves of the absolute beauty of things at the atomic, moment-by-moment end of the spectrum. Your breathing will change. Your muscles may give up some of their tightness. Your body may realign.

The As will wait for you. And you will be more ready for them when you come back with your focus so much the clearer for the time you spent with the *Aaaahhhs!*

Bleep!

This has to be the all-time best "unword." If I had exercised the wisdom to use it, there are a few times that things could have gone much smoother for me. There was that "Bleep you!" that I had the misfortune to *not* use one Thanksgiving at my parents' place. And "bleep" would have come in handy for my son on the playground in third grade. As it was, he faced the disgrace of suspension at a very tender age and a reputation for coming from a less than desirable family. It put a real damper on subsequent Boy Scout outings and party invitations, let me tell you.

My encounters with moments when "bleep" is a lifesaver have caused me to see that there are some downright incendiary phrases in the English language. And it's a bleeping good idea to clear them out.

Still, it's a shame to lose something that is so power-packed. So how about we take the ***oomph*** behind these troublemakers and give them a new life as little juicy phrases?

First, take me at my word and leave all the bleepable words out of the picture. Then find some juicy, power-packed words you like. Make up a nice set of phrases and then use them on yourself. Some of my personal favorites are:

You are truly amazing!
You do that incredibly well!
You are the best!
I know you'll figure that out!
Nothing stops you!

Now insert them in your day. You can get going early by working them into the AM bathroom routine. This gives you the advantage of looking yourself right in the eye as you say them. You can make it a silent, sort of inner recital if you want to avoid stares from others in the vicinity (dogs think you are talking to *them* and love the attention, however) or if you haven't mastered talking when your toothbrush is engaged.

Traffic jams are a great time for little juicy phrases. You will go completely unnoticed with others around you muttering under their breath as well. The difference is you'll be getting so much more out of your traffic moments.

It might feel a little stupid at first, saying things like this. I thought I would be above being so blatantly manipulated by my own self when I started playing with little juicy phrases. But you know what? I'm as gullible as the next guy. They really work on me! I have actually caught myself saying, "Thanks for the compliment" to *myself*, of all people. Out loud, once or twice.

Try tailoring a set of little juicy phrases for a project you're working on. Like if you are late a lot, make a set of phrases affirming your ability to be in the right place at the right time.

Or if you hate any particular day of the week, like Mondays or Wednesdays, do a set just for that day. Say nice things about the day. If you trash it, the day will not get better. Like, instead of "Monday bleeps! I can't believe the weekend is over and I am back at this bleeping job! I hate these bleeping Monday meetings! How am I ever going to survive until Friday??!!!" go for "Wow! A whole new week is starting! I can't wait to talk about my plans for the week! I'm going to be at my best this week! The sky's the limit!"

Okay, the sky part was probably over the top. But enthusiasm is a good thing. Be sure to put some in there for yourself. The only person who can possibly be embarrassed is you, right?

Are you wondering if you won't get wise to yourself after awhile and start canceling your little juicy phrases as fast as you make them up? Probably not. We like these dorky pats on the back better than horses love sugar lumps. Successful advertisers figured this out long ago. So why not turn into your own biggest backer?

Challenge, Choose, Changes

C is one of the richer letters of the alphabet. We could do choice (as in free), change/changes, challenge, centered, complete, chocolate.

As in creamy, rich, dense. Cookies, hot cocoa, cake with thick moist frosting, fudge, truffles, pudding, pie, *oh my!*

We may now be at one of those junctures where the needle scrapes across the record and we come screeching back to where we planned on going in the first place: to the *challenge* of working from our *centered, complete* self when we could easily choose to be dragged off by all the stuff that whirls around us, tornado fashion.

It takes real guts to stay on track with so much spinning in our heads. For example, think about how many voices are in that tornado in our head—expressing opinions about what we can and can't do with our lives. And what we should do.

The voices can come in early and stay for a long, long time. It can start with parents or brothers and sisters voicing their feelings about us. It can be expectations laid on us. Our family wanting us to fill a role. The family history demanding that we fit in the mold. Even the place where we grew up can lay expectations on us. Not to mention what we encountered at school, with the role we played with our friends, the feedback we got from our teachers.

Sheesh! Now that you think about it, doesn't it make you want to stand up and shout *"Back off!"* to the lot of them?

You could, of course, be extraordinarily compassionate about the situation and say that it doesn't hurt to be given a sense of direction and that the challenges each role presented helped you to grow enormously.

But I say let's can that and take some time out to identify those voices and their messages. Let's see what you like and what you could live without. If you're fifteen or fifty-five or three hundred and three, you can get a lot from doing this.

Get out the notebook!

You'll want to have a notebook for this. I have some exercises to help identify your voices. We're going to start with a

couple of ways to clear out the stuff you don't want and absolutely don't need.

What got embedded?

Over time, voices can change from things that were said to you to things that you now say to yourself. You might even assume that they are your own ideas by now and you may not recognize them as voices at first. If they're the kind that feed you and make you stronger, it's not such a big deal to be unaware of them. But if the voices are carrying messages that are getting in your way, you definitely want to find them and replace them.

Look for thoughts that drop in like, "I'm no good at this, why even try?", "I'm so clumsy, I break everything I touch!", "Every time I care about something, it turns to turds!", "If people knew how incompetent I really am, they'd never trust me!", "Sooner or later, I'm going to screw up!"

Yuck!! This stuff is poison! Get it out of your head! Write these poisonous statements in your notebook with a space next to each one so that you can re-write it. You are going to take the core idea, pull it out of the muck, and frame it in words that lift you, not drag you down. Like this:

I'm no good at this, why even try?	Each time I do this, I learn more and get better at it!
I'm so clumsy, I break everything I touch.	I take my time and handle things gently. That way I can enjoy them even more.
Every time I care about something, it turns to turds.	When something matters to me, I give it the time and attention it needs.
If people knew how incompetent I really am, I know they'd never trust me.	I can be trusted to do my best. If I need help, I know how to ask for it.
Sooner or later, I'm going to screw up!	If I make a mistake, I can admit it and learn from it.
Nobody listens to me or cares what I think.	I speak up for myself. When I have an idea, I share it.

Once you have the replacement statements ready, be on the lookout for your poison statements. As soon as one comes up, zap it with your new, lifting statement.

For an extra boost when you start the replacing process, write the new statements down in your planner, make little signs you can post by your mirror and on your computer monitor. This way you can see the lifting statements before the poison statements can even get started.

A common thread I find in poison statements is the impact they have because of the amount of emotional charge they contain. When we shift to statements that lift us, we are also changing our emotional fuel from those gut-wrenching negative, drag-you-into-the-pits blasts to something with the power to steady and carry us. So instead of living in fear that soon someone is going to discover how truly incompetent you are and looking for ways to, as they say, C.Y.A., you can be putting energy into improving your already excellent performance.

"When you grow up you're gonna be . . ."

Did your family have plans for you? What has happened to those plans? Did you bow to the expectations, or did you rebel and choose your own road? Do "I should have . . ." thoughts come up for you? Either because you felt blocked by your family and wish you had gone in your own direction, or

Take a look
at what
you have

been taking
for granted.

because they were right in the first place and you should
have followed the family's advice?

This kind of voice nagging at you is an energy
sapper. It's time to release yourself from the should-
haves—worse than the flu!—with a ritual if you're
game. Goes like this:

- Choose a time and place where you can be quiet
  and uninterrupted. Planning in advance will give
  you a chance to gather all your regrets, just in the
  back of your mind, so you can bring them to this
  ritual.

- When you are in that quiet time and place, give
  yourself some moments to settle in. Use whatever
  techniques you prefer to draw your thoughts to
  your center; calming music, slow deep breathing,
  a lighted candle for focusing.

- Now invite those nagging should-have voices to
  come forward. Write them on a sheet of paper
  as they come in. If you like to really get into
  rituals, select two sheets of colored paper and a
  pen and set them out before you begin your
  centering process. Use the first sheet for this step.

- When all the "should haves" are written down, thank these voices for their desire to help you and acknowledge their concern for your well-being. Tell these voices that you do not want their help. Tell them you have gained from the path you have chosen. Tell them that you do not regret the choices you have made, even when those choices were not perfect.

- Take a few moments to forgive yourself for choices that you view as mistakes, that you see as causing you losses. Remind yourself that you were doing the best you could at the time.

- Now tear the sheet of paper into small pieces. Burn the pieces if you can. If lighting them up would create a hazard or set off a smoke alarm, dispose of them. As you do this, tell yourself that you are now released from these thoughts, they are no longer a part of you.

- Take a second sheet of paper and write down everything you gained from living out the choices you have made. This one you keep.

Whew! Those first two exercises are the heavyweights in this process to choose the voices that support our **centered, complete** selves. It's time for something lighter.

Q&A

Let's move on to do some reflecting on some other sources of voices. These would be the messages we give ourselves about who we *naturally* are, when what we *naturally* are is really what we have learned to be.

This is a Q&A session. More note taking.

What We All Could Do

"In my family, we all have a knack for _____."

In my family, it was mostly a knack for telling stories. As kids we could come up with some fabulous, well, lies. Now that we have refined our skills, and learned to stay in closer proximity to the facts, we're all good storytellers.

I'm guessing that you told some whoppers along the way too, and maybe you didn't turn out to be a great storyteller. So what made the difference for me in my family setting? What became a "knack" of mine was a tradition of telling stories to get a message across that I learned from listening to my father and grandmother. And from trying out a tale or two myself and getting feedback.

If it was a good story, my audience stayed with me. If it was too far out, I got the equivalent of the old vaudeville hook—"Now Maureen, that couldn't be true." I was treated to the little shepherd boy and the wolf story several times, as a matter of fact. My Dad told it very well.

Take a look at what your own family setting taught you so early and so gradually that it has become your family's hallmark. Are you all great dancers? Do you sing at the drop of a hat? Do you all do calculations in your head? Do you make to-die-for peach preserves? Take a look at what you have been taking for granted. These are gifts you can use now to your advantage if you choose to build on them.

Everybody Has a Job

What jobs or chores were given to you? I was assigned to assist in lawn care, which got the title of Doo-doo-Nosed Pooper Scooper bestowed upon me by my brother. It didn't provide much inspiration for my future development, but as I mentioned, not every section of this little Q&A session is going to get results. In *your* case, however, you may have picked up (so to speak) some usable skills. Are you still using them? Or are there things that you don't attempt now because that was someone else's job in your family?

All Together Now!

What kinds of things did you do as a family? Did you play sports? Did you go to concerts? Did you travel? Did you spend time with relatives? What kinds of things do you do now? If you had the choice, what would you have wanted your family to do? What would you choose now? Are there gaps you would like to fill? Have you built things into your life today because it was what your family always did? Do they work for you, or do you want to re-vamp them or even throw them out?

School

What goes on at school can be entirely different from what happens at home. I'm sure there are theories about why this happens. The input from teachers and classmates or even the change in setting are pretty clear differences from your home life. In some cases, they seem to compensate for what is missing. In others, they can be a hugely painful experience. For the sake of recognition, make a "plus" list and a "minus" list of how you were viewed at school. Let all the voices have a say. Friends, enemies, teachers. Do one more thing: Recognize that at that point in our lives we were, without fail, works in progress. And next to every statement (plus or minus) give yourself an updated view of who you are.

Where Do You Come From?

You've known that for years, right? Okay, but after the birth event, did you come from a village or a city? How did the people in your village or city view success? Was everyone supposed to stay at the same level, or was outstanding achievement accepted? Did people say things like, "Nobody likes a show-off" or did they organize parades to celebrate local heroes? Did you feel like you fit in or did you feel like you would have to move away from home to get where you wanted to be?

Choose a Hero

Who were your heroes when you were younger? Who are your heroes now? You need one of these in the mix of the voices you choose to keep to give you something to hang onto in the tough moments.

And keep a family member in mind when you make your choice. There's special power in saying, "If Aunt Gloria could do it, so can I!"

For me, right after Superman on my heroes list (it was the flying thing that got me) comes my Aunt

Pat. My uncle died when the youngest of their six children was five, and the estate laws passed the family business to the children, not the widow. So Aunt Pat took on the double duty of raising her kids and running the business for them. When the family was grown and she could turn the business over to her son, she won a seat in the state legislature just so she could change the inheritance laws to guarantee that no widow would face what she had to ever again. Aunt Pat got the changes through in her third term in office.

My Aunt Pat is the most loving, accepting, genuine, fun, tough-as-nails person I have ever met. Whenever things get a little crazy for me, I think of her and my impossible-looking stuff shrinks back down to a doable size. Pick a hero for yourself and let her or him speak when you have the need.

Taking Stock

Now step back and take a look at what came out of the Q&A session. Did it shake out some of those messages you give yourself? Are the messages lining up with who you, as your centered, complete self *chooses* to be? Are there changes, adjustments you want to make? Voices you want to add? Voices that don't serve you that you want to eliminate?

It is in our hands to make these choices. The process has begun simply by allowing for the insights these exercises offer. What happens next can be a series of shifts in perspective. Subtle, under the surface changes.

If you find that stating your new choices in writing fits for you, go all out. Get some slick-looking paper to copy them on. Make it as creative and personalized as you can. The "Yes!" you give to your new choices will be planted even deeper for you and will support you without you having to be aware they are. And it will be much easier to be the centered, complete self you choose to be.

Drama Queen

Know any? Simple things like the quarter getting stuck in the parking meter or the check not arriving in the mail transform them. They can weep over too much salt in the soup for an entire meal. A ten-minute wait at the tollgate might as well be several lifetimes. Life is just plain larger for a drama queen.

I had a dog once who was a Drama Queen. You looked at her cross-eyed for wolfing down a whole cube of butter (how *did* she get on the counter that fast??) and she'd crank out a howl to chill the spines of neighbors for blocks around. But when that dog was happy, she could make her eyes glow. Ask her if she wanted to go for a walk (She had a pretty extensive vocabulary—walk, cookie, and supper were at the top of her list. She also understood "No!" and "Bad girl!" but she never really let it get in her way.) and she would rocket around the house and dance in front of the door with those eyes on mega-bright and her tail whipping fast enough to turn cream into butter. You just had to be charmed.

And that's the thing about drama queens that makes me wish I could be one—they know how to squeeze the max out of every moment of their lives.

With just a little tweaking, this drama queen, shall we say, ability, could make the same-old stuff in our lives take on new, richer meaning.

Let me begin with a disclaimer. If you go for the "My life *couldn't* be more miserable!" end of the drama queen spectrum, your friends—and maybe even nodding acquaintances— are going to cross to the other side of the street when they see you coming.

I'm not saying that there isn't a place for giant bursts of misery if you enjoy that kind of thing, but it's best practiced out of the range of sentient beings. Well, maybe plants or your cat can deal with it. Your human friends are going to notice right away that you're over the top. Mostly you will find the room has been vacated by the time you've finished your blast.

But drama queens know how to get madly excited about things in a contagiously cheerful way as well. They know delight inside out and backwards, and that's where the fun comes in. And where we're headed: ***Drama Queen for the Day!***

I like planning ahead. So I suggest you take a look at your calendar and choose which day of the month you will be Drama Queen for the Day.

Mark the day with a reminder to yourself in code. There's less to explain this way. You could use "DQD," or draw a star, or a balloon. You could use a highlighter to mark the date. You  could use a code word. Keep it simple enough so you don't forget why you put it there in the first place. Like if you went for "Hot diggity dog!" it might look like a lunch suggestion to you later on in the month.

So your DQ day arrives! Open to the possibilities! Let yourself look at every single ordinary thing from a true DQ perspective! The air is fresher than fresh when you breathe in a big gulp of it as you **launch** out of bed. The coffee couldn't *possibly* be more fragrant! The cereal was *never* crispier!

"It's going to be a *remarkable* day!" you proclaim as you head out the door. And you make it one just by your shift in focus.

Challenge yourself to observe what changes for you when you spend the day in DQ mode. Do you find you have a little more energy than usual? Is it easier to find the good side of stuff? Do people respond differently to you? Do the daily grind parts of the day seem less grinding?

If you find that you can make the day just a bit bigger and brighter and you enjoy your Drama Queen persona, consider adding the DQD to your bag of tricks. Then you'll have it handy when you hit a long slow period that looks like it's going on forever and you need a lift. Or use a DQD to give yourself some breathing space and help get you through the toughest part of a bad situation.

If later on, you discover little sparks of DQ popping up without you even thinking about it, consider yourself transformed—in the *best* possible way, of course. Any Drama Queen could tell you that.

Envelopes

You can stick in important stuff and seal and stamp them and send them off to somebody you care about.

You can get back in the good graces of your credit card company with them. As long as you put the check *behind* what needs to show through that tiny window.

You can get red ones stamped with gold letters and money gifts inside.

When we were just starting with envelopes, somewhere around kindergarten, we got little ones with no glue on the flap and a shadow of the valentine showing through.

If you have a certain kind of patience, you can make one of your own.

If you have no patience and you haven't gotten caught up in any crazes to be terribly chic and original, you can get them by the hundreds at any discount store.

And we all come with one. This could be news for a lot of folks who might remember being *enveloped in* something. Like love, for instance, when the valentines were delivered. Or fear when the grades came out.

Truth be told, we have a protective barrier that we can put into use any time we like. We can let in what we choose and let it surround us and feel enveloped in it. Or we can decide not to let something cross that boundary.

Mostly people seem to be haphazard about how they use their envelope. They throw it up around them if things aren't looking good and further input would be painful. So if you are getting really bad news and you feel yourself reaching the point of being overwhelmed, the things people are saying to you stop making sense. It's like the information doesn't get through any more.

Or you can be so full of something really great there isn't room to take in anything else. Like when you are listening to absolutely fabulous music, or you are completely touched by someone, or you are taking in a sunset.

You could say that when we get to the extremes, our envelopes are definitely active. A kind of automatic protective barrier. When we're bombarded with so much stuff that we'd lose ourselves if we took any more in, the envelope goes up around us and cuts off the input.

How about in situations where bombardment is at a level that's low enough not to be noticed? The envelope isn't on autopilot anymore. It may not even be activated. If you get to the end of a day that looked pretty ordinary and you feel absolutely drained, it's a good sign that you aren't using your envelope.

As if you knew that you could, right? You come with an envelope, no assembly necessary and *no instructions*!

And I'm itching to tell you how you can use it.

There are a couple of concepts that will make this explanation go smoother: First, consider that your envelope is made of an elastic kind of stuff that completely surrounds you. Kind of like someone blew a big bubble of bubble gum around you. Second, imagine that even though your envelope is made of an elastic kind of stuff and is like a big bubble around you, thoughts and emotions can still pass through it. Third, view all thoughts and emotions that come through your envelope as energy.

Now that you have these concepts, take some quiet moments to sit with this. And play a little.

The Energy Envelope

- Imagine your energy envelope around you.

- Notice how large it is.

- Play with the size of it, bringing it in close, and then expanding it out away from you.

- Make it as large as you can.

- Now bring it closer to you so that it is a comfortable size.

- Notice the texture of its surface.

- Notice if your envelope has a color.

- Notice if the color changes.

Your envelope is a very sophisticated device. It can be completely sealed, like a big balloon around you. It can be set up to let in only certain types of energy and can be programmed to cause other types of energy to bounce off and away from you.

Simply put, you can set up your envelope to let in only positive energy and to keep out harmful energy that would cause stress. It can be set up to let in energy that uplifts and supports you and to keep out energy that would drain you. What's more, you can arrange to keep out anyone who would take energy from you and deplete you.

How do we get these things to happen? By activating the mechanics of our envelope—changing the surface to let in what we want or block out what we don't, choosing what energy we want to fill it with, using it as a protective barrier to keep from being drained.

The activator is our imagination.

The Activating Process

- Take a few moments to get calm and centered.

- Gently focus on following your breath as you breathe in and out, slowly and deeply.

- Now place a soft focus on your envelope. Using your imagination as a sensing device, notice how far it is away from your body. Notice its texture and color.

- Choose how you would like to program your envelope (negative remarks bouncing off and away or letting in uplifting and supporting energy, or being completely filled with love, confidence, wisdom, etc.).

- Holding that intention, allow your envelope to adjust to this setting.

I suggest you choose just one item to program into your envelope when you begin using it. And touch back in every now and again during the day to renew it.

After some practice, you'll be able to add more elements. Or you may find that there are times you like having one clear, strong focus for your envelope. Feel free to explore. It is, after all, the envelope you came in.

Fresh!

Do you sometimes get the feeling that you have a dirt cloud around you? Not the kind that hits you on a dusty road, but a smudgy, heavy, emotional kind of a cloud. Like some weird kind of dust storm kicked up stuff and it's now swirling in your emotional airspace? It blocks your view and makes you feel like you've got grit in your eyes? Like the debris left from a bomb blast. Chunks and fragments of thoughts and feelings, not attached to anything you could name, just floating around loose.

It can be a sense of heaviness about you, making you feel just a little off. Or it can be so thick that it feels like you are smothered in it.

You are remembering when your coach would tell you to just shake it off after you were whacked off your feet.

But this stuff just will not shake. It sticks, even. It is nameless stuff that will not let go.

It doesn't work to reason your way out of something like this. It truly is beyond reason. You need to lift it off.

Not by sheer, teeth-gritting determination. By going out and above it. **Getting fresh.** Feeding on what is light and whole, not on this fear residue.

All you need is a doorway. The rest will follow without your effort. So you can be nourished and freshened. Lessen the length of the heavy moments. Dissipate their density. Help yourself to feel stronger, more able. Ready to take on the world again.

What does a doorway look like? It can be a change in your physical position, a slow, deep breath, the sounding of a note. Your doorway can take just seconds to access. Or if you have the luxury of time, you can make it a slow, full experience. You can change it from day to day to suit your changing situation. Play with a few choices and see what works best for you.

Here are some to get you started:

Finding a Doorway

Float Out

Take three slow, deep breaths and let your focus float out on them until the simple act of breathing carries you into a place of peace. I use "place" here not

Fresh! 45

to mean a physical space, of course. You're still in the room; just your focus is in another place. A softer, more nurturing one.

Make this shift a gentle one. Go for just the right amount of soothing, re-generating energy.

Stay with this until you have a sense that you have gotten what you need. And let yourself come back into the room just as gently. Notice how much lighter you feel.

Fresh, even.

I close my eyes to do this. And I come back to this doorway off and on during the day, whenever I feel the heaviness returning.

Stretch Yourself

Make all your body parts feel long and loose. Stretch arms, legs, back, neck, shoulders, fingers, toes. Be like a cat waking from a sunbath. Long, languorous stretches with a yawn at the end.

Get Warm Inside

Brew yourself a hot cup of tea (okay, coffee). Cup your hands around it. Take small sips. Say, "Umm!" to the taste. Take another swallow and follow it all the way down. Feel warmed, refreshed.

Stare

Out a window, into empty space. For as long as you like.

Play Music

Pick a piece of music that speaks just to you. One that begs you to get in there with it. Far enough in to feel it humming out your feet. When you play it, do whatever it invites you to do.

Get Smelly Flowers

Go to a flower shop and stick your nose in the bouquets. Never mind the colors and the shapes. Find something that smells great to take with you. Put them up close to your nose so the petals tickle. Take it all in, the fragrance, the soft petals on your skin. Then put them in a vase close to you so you can go back for more any time you choose.

Rub Shoulders

Find someone to trade shoulder massages with. If you've got a crowd of more-or-less friendly people around you, make a chain with them and let everybody get the kinks out.

Get Poetic

Read a poem out loud. Poems are word music. Give your voice to one. It will carry you out with it.

Weather

Go out in it and take it as it comes. Turn your face to the sun. Or stand in the wind. Or rain. Or catch snowflakes on your tongue.

Note that these are things that are easily within reach. Getting away for a day or a weekend is great, but we need doorways that are more immediate so we don't have to put off lifting out of the heaviness to a "better" time or place. We can use that doorway right when we need it. And be fresh again.

Ground(ed)

She's really grounded. He's got his feet on the ground. Underground, the place where you go when you want to be out of the line of fire.

Funny how we like to use the earth as our stable point. We expect it to be solid, predictable. Just like someone who's grounded, who keeps both feet in firm contact with the earth. Not like airheads. Or bird brains.

I see a message behind this. It speaks to me about an understanding we have that the earth offers strength. We can soak it up just like plants do. We might not have the benefit of roots, but we can still pull in that nourishing, settling energy and let it replenish and refresh.

When the daily balancing act gets off kilter and stuff seems to be spinning out of control, earth is a great place to go. Back to feeling the ground under our feet.

I like to get grounded by stripping off my shoes and getting soil or sand right down between my toes if I can. The world seems to calm for me as soon as I get myself planted.

If there isn't a chunk of earth handy, or getting down to bare feet would likely draw a crowd, I improvise. I use the old memory bank to call up a stretch of sandy beach, maybe, or a garden with the deepest, richest loam. Warm from the sun, groomed by the wind. I close my eyes and put myself there. I breathe deep and slow. I let calm circulate. I restore.

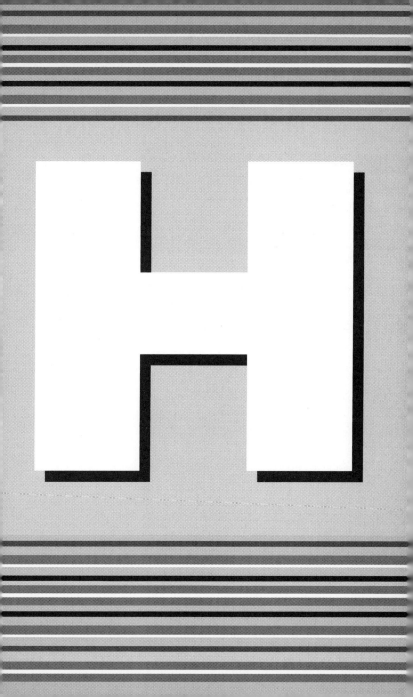

Hope and Healing

H & H. One H isn't enough. One is for hope and the other is for healing.

If you have faced a tragedy, if you have lost someone or something you cared about dearly, it is hope and healing that will see you through.

Without hope, you can head straight for bitterness. Without healing, despair and worse–revenge. And revenge is a sure road to sorrow.

I'm not talking about the hope where you cross your fingers and wish. I'm looking at stronger stuff. A belief that good can be buried in even the worst situation. It puts you on the lookout for those good points. They are the seeds, those small, comparatively unimportant good things hidden among the bad.

It comes down to a question of what we want. We have the say-so in this. The shock and the fear may be the first things to come in, but they don't have to be what we choose to live in. We have more to work with.

Feed the good things you've found and they'll be what comes up out of the tough times, not the stuff that gnaws at your gut and keeps you up at night.

It might feel shaky at the start. Standing in the path of a tornado after it has passed and noticing how much more of the sky you can see now that the buildings are blown down doesn't sound like much. After all, only a fool would stand there gawking at the sky, with their life lying trashed at their feet. Like turkeys that stand out in the rain with their heads up and their beaks open until they drown. (Ask any turkey farmer—this really happens!) But it's that spark we're after.

It's the small shimmers of hope that let us move forward. They leave less and less room for rolling around in the pain and pity. Even if we've earned it. Hope makes that second oh-so-critical H possible.

Hope is what heals.

Inside

Past the surface, into the heart of the matter, out of the cold, where the info is.

Aren't we always looking to get there? And aren't we careful to guard ours? I mean, if we let something or, **yikes!**, someone get inside us, we're invaded. We're exposed! Vulnerable! What if we have all this messy stuff going on inside? Not pretty! Maybe we'd like to do a little sprucing up before we let the world see us. Maybe we'd like to spruce up a bit before we let *us* see us.

If any of this is ringing a bell, it's time to take action. Getting comfortable inside our skins is action item #1.

There is a challenge here; I am not coming from the school of feeling free to be as snarly and obnoxious as you like and loving and accepting yourself for it.

I'm talking about being boldly, courageously honest inside. It includes admitting being horrid or dishonest or the world's greatest procrastinator or whatever other baggage we might be hauling around—and then asking ourselves what we are going to do about it.

Getting honest and feeling guilty gets us nothing. Okay, with the guilt you could have a really nice crying jag and a quart of French vanilla with triple thick chocolate fudge sauce. (This is mine. Yours could run in another direction, but we're ending up in the same place.) Getting honest and doing something about what we don't like is the deal.

This is big and could take some time. If you feel it's really big, get help. Life will be much lighter if you're happy with what's going on inside.

I want to give you some inspiration along the way. Here's a set of what often gets called affirmations. Quick hits to help firm you up and keep you on track. What you do with these things is first write each one on a separate piece of paper, like the fortune in a fortune cookie. Find a nice box to store them in. Then you can pull one out and read it to yourself when you need a boost. One a day if that works for you.

I am gentle with myself.

I take time to hear the beating of my heart.

When I feel angry, I let that anger flow past me like
a river. I let peace fill my heart.

I feel my inner strength.

I think clearly.

I never need to rush.

I reach today's goals easily.

Tomorrow's goals are for tomorrow.

I breathe in peace, I breathe out fear.

I trust my heart.

It is easy for me to laugh.

I am open to being loved.

I forgive, and let go.

I will give myself one small gift today.

Today, I take five minutes to sit in silence with just
myself.

I invite happiness into my life.

I let sadness be healed.

I count my blessings.

Today, I will help something to grow.

Jumpin' Jupiter!

Jazz joints and joy rides!

Jonquils, johnny-jump-ups, jack-in-the-pulpits!
Jasmine, pink and white and night-blooming!

Jawbreakers, jellies, and ***jambalaya!***

Jokes and jesters!

Giants and giraffes! (You have to spell them with a
G, but we all know better.)

Then there's justice and judgment.

You can go either way with J.

I say live on the light side.

Justice and judgment can take
care of themselves, we don't need
to worry ourselves with doling
them out.

Kick

K is the funny letter. In the 1960s, on the ground-breaking *Smothers Brothers* television show, Tommy Smothers used it in his act—he would make a *"k"* sound and look sly and everyone would bust up. A little tip—try it sometime at a party when conversation gets slow. Instant laughter. Unless it's mistaken for an expression of things not being quite right upstairs.

Once again, what's life without risk?

Everyone's #1 favorite K word is kiss. Hands down, it wins. I'm going for #2. Kick. People have even made careers out of kicking. If you've ever had the pleasure of putting all your force behind a perfectly aimed kick and blasting the ball to Never Never Land, you know why.

What's
life

without

risk?

We just seem to be made to kick. It's what we do when we're feeling frisky. We kick up our heels. When we're feeling strong, invincible even, we kick ass. When we're feeling generous, we kick in. When we need to concentrate harder, we kick it into high gear. When we absolutely to the core love something, *it* gives *us* a kick. When we need more help, sometimes we kick it upstairs.

And then, when we don't like what we've done, we could kick ourselves. Argh! If you've got that one in your repertoire, get out your big eraser and get to work! No more, I'm telling you! Didn't your mother say to be selective? Don't be taking the first kick that comes along. Wait for the good ones.

I'm serious about this eraser thing. We need a big pink rubber one—in our mind's eye. Otherwise it would be taking up space in our backpack or briefcase or whatever else we use to haul stuff around. Minds have much more room.

At the first sign of that nasty hangdog kicking-yourself feeling, ERASE!!! Until there's not a trace left. Then follow Dr. Maureen's prescription for getting on with your life:

- Acknowledge that things didn't turn out the way you hoped. If they didn't turn out right and other people are affected, give them your apology. Not, of course, an excuse. They'll be in no mood for

that. If they want you to do something to make
it right, accept graciously. And do it.

- Give yourself points for trying. We learn from
trying. There's power in that. We don't learn from
kicking ourselves. It makes us feel weak and turns
our attention away from what we could learn to
make things better next time.

- Do you hear a list coming? Oh, yes. Make a list of
everything you've learned. Everything from don't
force the key until you're sure it's really the right
one to checking that your cell phone is on your
side of the door in the first place. And need I
mention knowing who you should call when you
do locate a phone?

- Unload. Find a sympathetic (preferably uninvolved)
ear and tell them how traumatic the whole thing
is. If you can find some humor to dig out of the
mess, it will help enormously. This is why an
impartial third party is an especially good choice.
If it was their wedding cake that slid out of the
box and across the back seat, they most likely
won't see the humor in it. And believe me, they
won't care about the speeding ticket.

- Recognize that you need some soothing. Finding the good in the situation—getting a little emotional release is moving in that direction. Your body and soul need some support as well. Take a warm bath, get bundled up, play gentle music, have a cup of calming tea. Coddle yourself with as much care as you can. When your breathing has become slow and regular and you are calm again, let yourself be embraced by the love you have had in your life. In all the ways it has come to you. Love stays with us, you know. Call it up now and let it fill you and restore you. Let it carry you for a while.

- Move forward. No re-playing. You are stronger and wiser and maybe more compassionate for the experience. Take these new tools and put them to work in what comes next for you. Kickin'! Right?

Lucky

Lucky shot, lucky number, lucky shirt. Good luck.

Hoping for it when the odds are against you. It comes in streaks, with no rhyme or reason. Some people seem to have a lot.

Most of us suspect we have been shorted in the luck department. The Irish have been awarded a monopoly on it, and it seems as unpredictable as their leprechauns. It doesn't have a goddess, it only rates a lady. And

she's as flighty as the leprechauns. But it can sure make things better when she comes along.

Wouldn't it be great if there was a way to get on a lucky streak and stay there? Casino owners would quake when you walked in the door. Dating would become a thing of the past. Stuff would just fall in your lap—jobs, winning lotto tickets, the new car from a drawing that had a gazillion other entrants, the best seats at the concert. A wild, fun, crazy ride, no doubt.

Are you waiting for me to tell you that it is actually possible to get in that good luck zone and stay there? I'm not going to—because we both know it's not possible. Besides that much luck could kill you if your friends didn't first. They'd all zoom right past green with envy and start glowing chartreuse.

I am going to say, however, that you can make your own luck. Making your own luck is just a matter of a little shift in perspective. Think of a lucky horseshoe and a magnet. Similar shapes. But one is charged with a weird kind of energy that attracts. In the scientific world, this only gets you iron particles. You take this magnetism concept to the imagination level and things can happen!

There are a couple of prerequisites to this little shift from luck to magnetism.

First, you have to take aim.

Make your own luck.

With magnets, you need to choose a target. You have to be clear about what you want. Different than luck, which just lands on you.

And then (and this is the part that takes some practice) that part of you that is so very fond of making wise choices has to be in agreement. It needs to be clear that what you want is really going to be good for you.

At least that has been my experience. Maybe that just isn't so.

Tell you what—I'm going to lay out how you can go about setting up a magnet and you play with it for a while and see how it works for you.

I recommend that you start with something on the "2 to 3" end and not the "10" end of the scale of something that you want, for starters.

The Magnetizing Process

- Set aside a few minutes when you can be quiet and focused and free of interruptions. Allow yourself to settle into that quiet space. Closing your eyes and following your breathing will, as they say, get you there.

- Now bring in an image of what you want to magnetize. (Remember—start with a 2 or a 3). Play with this picture, making it as complete as you can. Check it out to make sure you have it just the way you want it. Make some adjustments to the image if it needs them.

- While it's sitting there in front of you, do a little tire kicking. Try it on for size in your imagination. Does it feel right? Do some comparison shopping—change your picture and see which fits you better, your first picture or the new one.

- If after you do this, your image doesn't feel comfortable, let it go. Because you will probably not be happy with it.

- Let's say this situation or thing you want is a "go." You have a nice clean image, it feels right for you. You are ready to turn your picture into a magnet.

- You start with a seed, a core, and then you are going to energize it, charge it up, just like a magnet gets charged. While you are in your quiet space, gently hold the image in your imagination and surround it with light. Choose a color for the light if you like. Let your image glow with the light for a few minutes as you hold it. And then let it go.

- Give yourself a few quiet minutes every day to do this. Hold your seed steadily in your imagination and envision it getting brighter and stronger. As you do this, you are actually charging it with your own energy.

- If you can, step back from expecting things to happen in a certain time or a certain way. Time in regards to this process is not something that can be marked on a calendar. Things are getting lined up on an energy level. It's like a winter soup—it needs to simmer. And you are doing a little simmering yourself. Just stay with the magnetizing process and let what happens happen.

Me! Me! Me!

Hey! Is that a good thing? I remember a person much larger than myself leaning over me and prodding me with, "Don't be so selfish, share! All the *good* girls are sharing."

Me first! Me! Me! ***Me!***

Bad! Bad! Bad!

I right away decided that bad is better. I'd go for keeping a whole cookie over only getting a half any day, any way.

I forgive myself for this. It was that first self-recognition phase of my life, and I needed me to come first.

Dare I say it? We all need "me" to come first. It's the way we clarify for ourselves and the world that we honor our needs and our boundaries. We need this—not knowing where we end and someone else begins screws up relationships. I'm not talking about the cookie-sharing kind of relationships. I mean *every* relationship—with our dog, our mother (not necessarily in that order), the mail carrier, a best friend, a lover, a coworker, a boss.

It's like this: If we lose sight of what we need to feel whole, we give too much of ourselves away. Then we begin to feel empty, to fall into need. We become a clingy, whiny, attention-grabbing, depressed, hypochondriac-prone mess. Okay, we can't manage to get that far overnight, but that's the track our train will be on. Or the optional track: angry, alienating, self-involved, mercenary, dishonest.

If the giveaway happens when we are very young and have not yet formed a healthy understanding of where that line between "me" and others should be, we may be running on one of those two tracks completely unaware. Like a low hum in the background that gets louder and more insistent as we fall deeper into need.

And then something that happens today triggers a memory of that first "giving away too much" event. So we might overreact. Like me and this thing I have about cookie sharing. Today, I do not share. I can bake dozens of cookies and happily give them away, but if I have marked a cookie as mine, held it in my hand, inhaled that rich, buttery cookie fragrance, I'll kill you if you so much as look longingly at it. Clearly I have a lot of shared cookies to make up for.

What if we find ourselves feeling like we've once again given away too much? Piteously empty where we should be full. Wrung out, flattened. Uncared about, unwanted. Or

It's time
to do
some refilling.

maybe taken for granted. Used like a doormat! We're ready to smash the next person to expect the tiniest thing of us.

This all sounds pretty grim. But it's really helpful. In a warning sign sort of way. If we notice ourselves going in one (or both! gawd!) of these directions, we are sending ourselves a signal—we lost track of our "me" boundary. We *are* empty where we should be full.

So we can relax and stop blaming the thoughtless insensitive demanding uncaring narrow-minded self-seeking uh, *jerks* (there are much better names to give them that I'm sure you can call to mind) around us and get down to business. It's time to do some refilling.

Amazingly, we are the ones who know best what this takes. It's cruel to expect someone we care about to figure it out for us. It's like asking the scooper at the ice-cream counter to tell you what flavor you want. You know you're allergic to peanuts and hate chocolate. Why make them guess and maybe send you into anaphylactic shock?

Speak up! Tell yourself you need care. Look right in your mirror and say, "You need to take care of yourself."

Just the act of switching from blaming everyone else for the way we feel and turning to ourselves instead will make a huge shift. It is the first step in refilling.

Even if it feels like you're one giant empty well that has been dry for so long you can't remember a time in your life when you have ever felt full, whole.

It could be so.

But then it could be that when the refilling begins the emptiness goes away. If it doesn't, you will want to take care of yourself by getting help.

Begin the refilling with a question. Ask yourself what you need to do to allow refilling to happen for you. If the first thing that comes up is a shiny new car or a ten-bag shopping jag or a bottle of Jack Daniels or an entire chocolate cake with a full inch of ooey-gooey frosting, you aren't filling your gaps, you're distracting yourself. You'll be staring down that same dry well when the high wears off.

Go for simpler with less wear and tear on your body and your bank account. Here are some choices that might work for you:

- Dust off some memories—times you felt whole, loved. Get out the family photo album and look for all the snapshots that show that love. Let yourself go back and fill up with those good times all over again.

- Sing. Pick a song that is especially rich for you and sing it out, full bore. I discovered this on a fishing trip when I was six. I was sort of improvising. The other folks up and down the river weren't impressed and neither were the fish, but it still felt great. Later, I tried it with the bell on my new bike as accompaniment. Same results all around.

- Clean something. Guys love to do this with their cars and bicycles. Makes them feel all fresh and new. Women seem to go more for a closet. I have no idea why this works. It's sexist, I know. But whatever.

- Do something nice for your body. Take it out for some exercise and air. Let it soak in a tub of warm scented water. Get it a good rubdown.

- Do something nice for your soul. Read it something that inspires it. Treat it to a sunset, a grove of trees, a blooming garden. Take it to a place of worship.

- Lose yourself for a while. Escape is heavily underrated. All kinds of refilling goes on when we stop paying attention to who and where we are. We can do it with a few moments of staring out a window. We can take more time and get involved in a story. A movie, a magazine article, a novel, some great gossip all work about the same.

- Make something. Cooking, growing stuff, building things, re-building things. Sewing, painting, throwing pots (that's a technical term for making stuff with clay, not bashing all the dishes in sight). Anything in those areas.

- Do something childish. Bubble blowing, kite flying, growing beans in a jar, starting an ant farm, playing favorite games. I've found that the results are much better when you've got some years behind you. It kind of makes up for the way things went earlier on, too.

If by now you have the impression that refilling is pretty darned uncomplicated and can fit right into the rest of your life, I don't mind in the least. As a matter of fact, that's the idea I'm after. Build in taking care of the "me" so that it can happen easily and you won't run into those crashing and burning times that are such a chore to work our way out of.

You might run into a by-product of all this "me-ness"—start doing some of your refilling with friends and you could turn into a fun person to be around. Even if you still haven't gotten over the cookie-sharing thing.

Notice

This is a magical thing. Somebody says notice, everything else stops. And we notice. We zone in. We become free from all else. Try it. Notice

your breathing
the air around you
the color blue
the feel of the sidewalk under your feet
the sounds of the street.

Instant Zen.

Open!

An oaflike ornery ogre ordered onions over octopus, outraging the overworked owner of the Open Oven, which offers onions only on ostrich omelets.

Just trying out my Os.

Out with this obviously off-track opening! And on to: **Open!**

We like open. All kinds of stuff can happen with "open." When we're open, we're letting everything come in, not shutting anything out. Not clamming up, keeping that mind open.

So, what if that ornery ogre plops its oaflike self down in front of you and demands you serve up something that turns your guts to glue just thinking about it? So much for open, right? That ogre's gonna be on his petoot in the gutter where all octopus swillers belong faster than an ostrich can blink.

Open is not so easy. We might not have ogres taunting us every day with their ugly, drooly faces. At least not literal ogres—we've got other stuff happening that can feel a lot like ogres and be just as off-putting. But we can learn a technique that helps keep us open in the face of ogres and other nasty stuff.

First off, look for your shutdown signals: anything from a frown and folded arms to stepping backward and mentally preparing to strike back. You can score them if you like. On a scale of one to ten, a creased brow is the one and shouting and ripping up paper is the ten. Somewhere in the middle is having a sudden urge to cover both your ears and ***hear no more!***

We can override the shut down and shift past that initial boiling point to an open exchange by offering a view of how we are feeling and what we need and making room for a response in that same vein. This is the beginning of a communication cycle that I'm going to show you how to use.

Here's the cycle:

- Honor your feelings. No stuffing. Accept them.

- Make an "I" statement, giving feedback on how you feel.

- Listen to the response.

- Make another "I" statement, giving back what you have heard.

- Make a statement of your needs and offer a suggestion of how your needs can be met.

- Listen to the response.

- Make another "I" statement, giving back what you have heard.

- Make another suggestion of how your needs could be met given this new information.

- Listen to the response.

- Continue with this cycle until you have an agreement. It could be a "yes" agreement, it could be a "no" agreement.

It looks something like this:

We are ready for our initial response. We allow it. We recognize it's made of a haze of emotional stuff. We can let that clear. And then we make our first response. "I feel uncomfortable hearing the price has gone up." There. It's out in the open. We kept those internal attack dogs tightly reined and still made our point. This might be "no" information we're getting, but it's an open response we're giving. So we can hear more. And again respond with another "I" statement. "I hear that your costs have gone up and this is the best you can do." Followed up with stating our needs: "I don't have that much in my budget this month. Would it be possible to spread out my payment over a longer period?" So, again we can hear more. And respond: "I understand that you need to cover your costs in the first month." And state our need: "What if I pay half now and then spread out the rest over the next two months?"

Sometimes a "yes" does come out of the interaction. We know it doesn't guarantee a "yes." It just leaves the door open. And if there isn't a "yes" that can happen now, the road is paved for open discussions later.

As far as the shutdown signals go, even if you didn't give yourself a score over three (and you're either doped up or in denial if that's the case), the cycle could make things run smoother for you. You'll be open and ready for anything. Even should some five hundred-pound beast come stomping through your door.

Pretend

It was the beginning of the best games. "Pretend I'm the king and everybody does what I say." "Pretend that we're in the jungle and all of the elephants and tigers give us rides on their backs." "Pretend that we're grown up and nobody can tell us when to go to bed."

People who sell cars know how much we love this game. "Pretend you've got this really hot car and you drive for miles and miles to the most breathtaking, exotic places." "Pretend your car can take you on fabulous adventures—across rivers, over mountains." "Pretend everyone admires you as you cruise around town in your shiny, luxurious car that screams money."

Notice something here? "Pretend" is saved for the good stuff. Nobody is interested in pretending that everyone hates the king and throws him out, or the elephants stampede and smash everything in the jungle. And who would want to pretend that her car gets stuck in the mud out there in the middle of nowhere? Or that your friends are so grossed out by how obsessed you are with your car that they stop speaking to you?

We want our fantasy to be fun. We want it to lift us up. We have an unending supply of reality to deal with. And it gives us plenty of opportunities to be bored or scared or frustrated. So fantasy is for the good stuff.

Adult pretending gets us ready to accept the good stuff, helps us to see the opportunities for the good stuff to happen, helps the people around us (who we're playing/pretending/living/working with) make room for the good stuff in our lives and theirs.

I'm not saying that pretending to win the lottery is a surefire way of coming up with the winning ticket. But thinking of ourselves as winners could have some pretty potent effects.

Pretending is a catalyst in a way. We want new good stuff, we need to draw it to us and get ready for the change that new good stuff brings with it. Pretending does that.

How this works is that a part of us is fooled by the pretending. At deeper levels, we believe the change has already happened. We begin to live like the change has happened. We begin to think and act differently. We begin to feel differently. We see things we would have missed before. We act on this new information. And people who hadn't seen us in the past could start taking notice.

We roll into the change and the opportunities that spring up so gradually that we may not notice our process. We could even be surprised when the new good stuff shows up.

There is an art to this kind of pretending, no doubt about it. It takes some practice. And a light touch. It's a lot like sending up balloons. Here's how it works, step by step:

Sending Up Balloons

- "What is your desire?" Can't you just imagine your own private genie poofing up before you and inviting you to state your request? Okay, so there's the genie. Make your request for the good stuff you want to happen as simply as you can, remembering how confused genies can get.

- Instead of turning your request over to the genie, you're going to send it up yourself. We just need to translate what we're after into a form that will be effective. And genie talk works best.

Send up
Send up
Send up

Send up

Send up
Send up
Send up
Send up

your balloon.
your balloon.
your balloon.
your balloon.
your balloon.
your balloon.
your balloon.
your balloon.

- Select a balloon. Imagine it to be a color and type that best fits your request. It can be mylar, it can be multicolored, neon, or "Red Balloon" classic.

- Blow your request into the balloon. Imagine your balloon filling with the thoughts and images you put together for the genie. Let the balloon fill up completely and notice that as it fills, it becomes more and more buoyant, lighter than air. Now tie it off tight so all your thoughts and images are sealed in.

- Send up your balloon. Imagine holding it up above you, feeling it tug against your hand. Let it go. Imagine it sailing up, riding the wind currents, carrying your request out to where it can be heard by the highest and best grantors of wishes.

- Send up more balloons. Once the first one is sent up, more of the same can be sent just by a quick recall of the first one you released. Try for one send-up every day for a couple of weeks. First thing in the morning is a good time to do it. If it begins to take effort to call up the balloon, it's time to stop.

Quicken

Yeah, that money management program. But "quicken" had a life before computers. It was what docs called that first sign a little being was bouncing around in a new mom's mushrooming belly. It was an especially intimate event, an initial contact between mom and baby. A reaching toward each other. So fleeting at first that it is hard to call real.

Things have changed since Quicken became a software program—now docs don't have to wait for moms to say, "I felt the baby!" They can use ultrasounds to get a view of the baby-to-be. Quickening displayed on a monitor. With a snapshot for Mom to take with her.

As fond as I am of baby pictures, I say it takes some of the romance out of the thing. First time baby knocks,

Mom says, "Yeah, I know you're there. I saw your picture." Not, "Oh my God! This is *real!*"

I'm sure if we took a poll of new moms, there'd be plenty that love the ultrasound and feel oh-so-romantic taking the snapshot home, showing off what looks mostly like a tadpole, and getting oohs and ahhhs galore.

So what's my beef?

Getting something new started is not so cut and dried. It can have a tenuous beginning. A questioning period and a slow period growing into the *idea,* never mind the *reality* of the thing. So it's the instant confirmation part that gets me. Losing the sense of the reaching out into uncertainty, living and breathing the hope and fear that comes with making something new.

Making isn't really what's going on. Growing is going on. That's what we humans continually do, you know. We do get to full size, of course, but we never really reach some ending point. Being grown up is just the fabrication of a frustrated parent trying to get their kid to stop bugging them—"Wait until you're grown up. Then you can drive cars, stay up until all hours, drink stuff that will make you throw up."

It's a messy business, growing. It's more of a zigzag, creation kind of event than the straight-as-an-arrow action the outside world is looking for. New insights, new ways of being are developing as we dive into new challenges. Just as tenuously as for any other growing thing. With periods of confusion and groping in the dark.

It's then that knowing about quickening can make all the difference—our secret weapon for counteracting doubts and fears. We can let go of a need for instant results. We can suspend judgment about outcomes. We are on the lookout for times when that chaos that is storming around us has a whisper of order and purpose. Quickening moments when we can touch in and feel the shifts we're making. Things that no one else can see for us.

So we can live with the gap between what the outside world wants to see and our own internal zigging and zagging. We can even put together punchy action plans full of our goals and strategies—and at the same time be comfortable knowing that what is driving the well-ordered picture we are presenting is the much richer, and sometimes messier, internal world of our own growing.

Recognizing those critical quickening moments is a personal business. We all have our own style. Here are some suggestions to try if you find yourself at a loss for a system that works best for you:

- Imagine that you have an internal signaling system that is attached to a sensor. The sensor picks up even the slightest "movement in the right direction" that you make. Set the volume control on the signaling system to a level that makes it easy for you to be alerted to those movements. You can program the signal that the system sends to be a clear but understated chime, trumpets, a voice that shouts "You've got it!", a chorus singing Handel's "Alleluia!", whatever works for you.

- Make an agreement with yourself that every time you make a shift, a discovery that can move you forward, you will be presented with a rose. The presentation could be a picture of a rose flashing in your imagination, imagining the scent of roses, a rose in a vase or in a garden catching your eye, a thought coming up of wanting to buy a rose. And if someone gives you roses, give yourself credit where credit is due.

- Go Las Vegas. Imagine that you have an internal Las Vegas-style slot machine with lights and bells that go off just like they do when you hit the jackpot. Only this jackpot is those quickening moments that you might otherwise overlook.

- Consider those quickening moments to be the same as "being in the flow."

Make an agreement with yourself that when they happen, you will have an experience of your thoughts and emotions, your essential being, flowing. Just like a huge, powerfully flowing river.

- This one is so overused that I hesitate to mention it: See the light bulb going on. If this works for you, by all means go for it.

Real

Let me tell you how things are in the real world. There is no room for deception in the real world. What is, is.

Until it changes.

So—what if our reality changes? What if the way our world runs and what we do in it, how we see things, takes a left turn and becomes something entirely foreign to us?

I grant you it's pretty unlikely that's going to happen. But do you want to take some time out and play "What If?" with me, just to try out what such a radical change in your life would feel like?

- It starts with a "What if___?" The "what if" is going to be something that looks unchangeable. Like "What if there is no such thing as only one right person for me?" "What

What is, IS.

if I had to live without knowing where my next meal was coming from?" "What if my beliefs are not the only 'true' beliefs?" "What if my children don't share my values?" "What if I didn't have a car?" "What if not having children is better for me?"

- If you haven't been able to come up with something and none of these ring a bell, choose someone who sees the world 180 degrees differently from you and try on one of their rock-solids.

- Live with the "what if?" for a week. What choices would you make? What issues would come up? How would the outside world see you? What would you say to the people who knew you before this change?

- At the end of the week, do some reflecting. Did living in the "what if?" for a week change your perspective on how you live your life? If the "what if" happened, would it change who you are? Would it change your relationships? Would it affect your priorities? Did the "what if?" you chose line up with a question you may have been wanting to ask yourself?

- If you gained something from your week, take time to acknowledge what that is. If you didn't, I congratulate you on your willingness to do something that definitely belongs on the loopy end of the reality spectrum.

- If you found yourself "walking a mile in another's moccasins," I hope the time spent there provided you with that most precious of gifts: honoring another's vision and embracing another's heart.

Some Super S Words

Sizzling! Remember that thing friends used to do—lick their finger and touch it to you and pull it back fast and make a sizzling sound—because you're so hot?

Smashing! The thing that Brits say when something is absolutely the best.

Superior. What stuffy people call more than excellent.

Star. You're shining up there!

Spirited. Great in racehorses, even better in humans!

Sagacious. When wisdom is just oozing out of you.

Sunny. Your side of the street.

Stalwart. When you're the steady, true blue you.

Swanky. Okay, maybe *slick* is better. Or *swoozie.*

Choose an S word or two to call yourself today. See if things don't just all seem to be somehow lighter.

Tortoise

Is it timeless? Tomorrow? Transcendental? No! It's ***tortoise!*** In honor of my dear friend, Larry, who stayed behind when his original owner—who is now in his twenties and has a hot car and a life but was twelve when Larry moved in—moved out.

It's been a reasonable arrangement for us both. We are at peace with our compromises. I with the fact that Larry is not furry and affectionate and Larry with the limits of a deck to range in.

Larry has finally remembered about the hazards of going over the edge of the deck when he comes out of hibernation. I think the thing that got it permanently planted in his tortoise-sized brain was an incident last spring when a pair of doves moved into the hanging planter out there. They hatched two chicks. No problem for Larry and fun for me. Then the chicks figured out they had wings and started working on their navigation basics.

It was one of those days when Larry, having lost some memory during his six months out of commission, forgot that when you step over the edge, you get wedged between the deck and the railing before you hit the ground. Then you have to hang there, stuck, until the human discovers you're missing and reaches down and hauls you out. Only this time the human looked and looked for Larry and could not find his hard-shelled, beady eyed little butt. She did notice that the parent doves had taken to landing on the deck and marching in circles, their heads bobbing in an oddly disturbed way. It's worth one more try, she thought, and got down on her hands and knees and looked deep over the deck edge. There was a gray puffball of feathers down there, and it had tortoise legs waving madly under it. Dove chick must have had a crash landing and broken its fall on Larry. So they spent the day together. Not happily for Larry.

He's got it now. You don't want to turn into a bird perch, stay *way* away from that deck edge.

And I—what I have learned is something about time and relationships. They don't hatch overnight like dove chicks. They are subject to trial and error. And they include making room for differences.

And being understanding about what matters, even when it's far from what is important to you. And that meeting eye to eye even when you're on very different levels can carry meaning you had no idea was possible.

Unite

Unite shows up in political slogans: "United we stand, divided we fall." Or "____united for____" like "Dogcatchers united for peace."

Unite is about strength, purpose, clear-sightedness. United celebrates the common cause. It takes the many and binds them into the one.

Unite is an internal thing as well. Because we are a bundle of levels ourselves. We've got personalities, lower selves, higher selves, bodies, minds, spirits.

In older religious traditions, unite was not the story. There was this division between the stuff of heaven and the stuff of earth, with heaven being a whole lot better. In my experience of one of those traditions, it was advised that we separate our worldly selves from our heavenly selves. The big stars were the folks who gave up all "earthly desires" to go for the gold. Like you could actually get a crown if you could hang in there long enough.

I'm coming dangerously close to the edge of impertinent irreverence, if not downright disrespect here. So let me take a few steps back and just say that it's no news that we live at multiple levels. Most times they all work together. We hardly notice that our one self is made up of parts. When they aren't so harmonious, we can experience something as mild as feeling off balance, out of sorts. If they're really off kilter, we can fall into deep depression. We can, as it is said, completely lose our sense of self. A very deep well to climb out of.

Before that very bad thing happens, let's set things up so we have somewhere to go to get things back humming. Let's say that the way we get our parts perking along together is to set up a core for them. Something to give them a point of reference. Then they can automatically re-orient themselves without us having to figure out how to direct them.

And now we find ourselves right back at the "worldly" and "heavenly" question. We need a power core, a receptacle that can hold and radiate energy and is capable of being replenished. We need something heavenly.

Far be it from me to say what that "heavenly" core should be. Organized religion seems to have been attractive to many. Wicca can work well. The Christian or Eastern traditions are possible choices. The more generic trend toward spirituality will do it.

Choose one that feels like a fit for you. Then work it. Just like muscles.

Our part in working our core is to spend some time and focus on replenishing. The model often used is to have a scheduled time and an organized fashion in which to replenish. Often in a group setting. Plain and simple— attend services. Or meditate.

I'm feeling a little apologetic about preaching in this way. I have never imagined myself as someone who would advise getting religion. But you know, we are heaven and earth beings. We've been working at doing this juggling act probably since humans got started. I have a sense that making a stab at getting the *this world/other world* thing to be in less opposition could save us all a lot of grief.

Maybe U should be "unicorn" instead—A meditation on a magical beautiful beast that comes to grace our troubled world. A moment of frothy fantasy to carry us away. Make our hearts lighter. Reflect back to us our wish for pureness and clarity. Oh, to ride a unicorn . . .

Vines

V is another animal story. It starts with a plant, a tomato *vine.*

In my mother's summer garden, there were always tomatoes. The vines would grow thick and lush, with tomato blossoms to burn. When the tomatoes "came in," as she said, they were unforgettable.

But the thing I loved most about those vines was hunting down the newly hatched hornworms among the leaves. Their bodies were a striking shade of translucent green and had a red spike sprouting up like a tail. A cut above the earthworms my mother thought so highly of, in my mind. I collected them in jars and fed them with leaves from my mother's vines. I carried them around the neighborhood with me to show off how fat they'd grown. I gave them earth to burrow in when

it was time for them to cocoon. And when huge moths broke out of the cocoons, I opened their jars and let them go.

It never occurred to me that my mother and I were working at cross-purposes. And she never let on that I was cultivating the very creature that preyed on her vines. It could have been that she thought there were more than enough tomatoes to go around. It could have been that I was having such a good time, she hated to spoil it. Either way, I love her for her tolerance.

If I were Aesop and this a fable, I'd say that no two people ever have the same vision, but still they can share the same vine.

Since I'm not, suffice it to say that it's good to go back now and again and remember what you might have been given along the way. And to put it down on paper just the way you remember it.

I invite you to spend a month letting those memories return and writing them down as they come in. Like my worm, er, vine, story. After which you have no need to feel any story is too small.

And if you're having a moment when you are feeling not at all rich, you can go back and read them to yourself.

If I were Aesop and this a fable, I'd say that then you will know you are very rich indeed.

Words

W has the honor of beginning some spectacular words—wish, winner, wonder, whisper. All top drawer. It also gets stuck with wanton, weird, wasteful, wuss, wilted.

Clearly it's a big player in the alphabet, and tying myself down to just one (pronounced *won,* don't you know) has taken it out of me.

I've decided to go with ***word,*** as it is at the root of what I do and where, after all, would I be without it?

It's come to my attention that words change radically when they go from spoken to written. That sticks-and-stones thing we chanted as kids does not apply at all to words on paper. Words on paper are a force. "Let's put that in writing" means people are getting serious. And we all know what signing our name at the bottom of the page does. Read the fine print, right?

Spoken words, the ones that stay in the air and never make it to paper, are another matter. We have a belief, some of us, that there have been times when speaking just the right word could make astounding things happen. We have felt them sting, or set our hearts to pounding. That putting words to a wish would be the thing that would cause it to happen. And a word given binds us.

It may be that those beliefs belong to an earlier time, or were only a contrivance of storytellers wanting to make their point.

Either way, we seem to have come to take it for granted that spoken words are harmless.

We don't believe that we could cause someone to drop dead because we said so. We'd be called simple if we believed someone had gotten their socks knocked off, had their eyes bulge out larger than their belly, or had alligators snapping at their shorts. To say nothing of the ridiculous possibility that a living breathing human would have body parts that could change into a foreign substance—legs to jelly, hearts to stones, the delicate and complex nervous system becoming the same stuff as mag wheels, or ice water pumping through a circulatory system. Just figures of speech, no more real than a wish made on a candle.

I'd like to tell you about an experiment with two bowls of rice in Japan where children spoke to one bowl of rice with hateful words, and to another with remarks about

Words on paper are a FORCE.

its beauty. The rice that received the hateful words became putrid, while the beautiful rice stayed just that.

What if the way it really works is that words spoken carry a piece of us out with them. Our force behind the meaning of the words. And that force is so significant that when our spoken words are recorded, they become as law.

I look at things this way and I become humbled and a little horrified. If I can put things out with my words that are more than just the words themselves, I can touch people in an extraordinary way. Hurtful or healing, depending on how I pick them.

It's not that I'm saying I'm going to be walking on egg shells. But when something really matters it might not be a bad idea to choose the words with the same care as if the message they bear for us could cause an action.

Just in case that's the way it really works.

X Marks the Spot

X rarely shows up at the start of a word. More often than not, it comes up after *e*—extra, exchange, exciting, exquisite, for instance. X seems to work better, be stronger in this little bond it has with *e*.

I see no reason to think less of X because of this. As a matter of fact, I think it speaks very strongly of the effectiveness of being in the background some of the time.

We mark our wins, our achievements. How about we try marking our moments of being the X. The times that without standing in the limelight, we are the instrument of something good happening. The times we make it possible for estranged friends to come together, for the traffic to flow more smoothly, for the mail to go out on time.

Why not put an X on our calendar for every one of those events—a big juicy one marking the spot?

It can be a matter just between us and X, no applause necessary.

Yosemite

I'd like this to be Yosemite. If you've been there it will be instantly clear to you why. Just thinking about it brings up images of mountains and forests and waterfalls that had to be originally designed to take your breath away.

If you haven't, it'll probably just remain an odd-looking unpronounceable word. No doorway to a few precious moments that have nothing to do with today, no reminder of where you've been and where you might go again. Just a string of not-so-meaningful letters.

I want to tell you if you don't get Yosemite, I hope there's some other place you *do* get. What's more, you need pictures of that place. Snapshots in your drawer. And you pull them out and riffle through them and let yourself go back there. Until your breathing deepens and the kink goes out of your neck and the corners of your mouth begin to turn up. And you feel just great about going back to today.

Zone

That narrow, elusive space where our minds are clear and time all but stands still. Where we feel no fear, can do no wrong. Where endless resources of insight and ability are at our fingertips.

If we're fortunate, we get flashes of this space. Always we want more.

Getting there one hundred percent and being able to stay there. We want that. Any athlete or dancer can tell you it doesn't happen without preparation and practice. But it is well within the range of the human experience, this zone. Not just the superstars have rights to it.

I offer a doorway to your zone for you to play with. Because the zone is a form of lightness, playfulness. Effort is not a doorway. Play is.

This is an exercise that is best listened to. Record it for yourself, or have someone read it to you. You will want

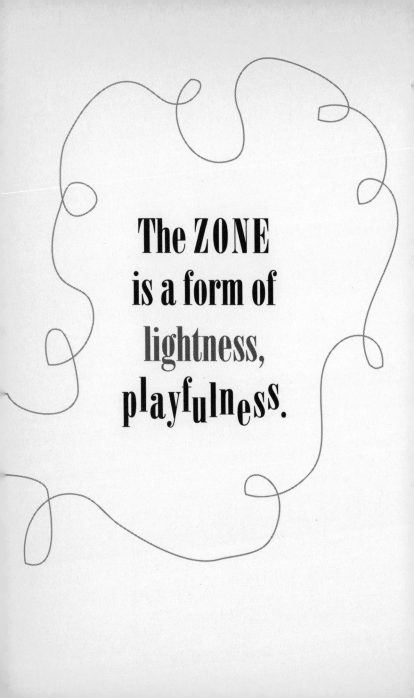

The ZONE
is a form of
lightness,
playfulness.

to slow down the pace of the reading and use the same kind of soft voice you would use to gentle a child to get the full effect.

The Doorway to the Zone

- Begin with noticing the pace of your breathing. Allow your breathing to slow as you follow it in and out. Now inhale slowly and deeply and hold the air in your lungs for the count of three. And breathe out just as slowly and deeply. Stop and count to three once again before you inhale. Inhale, slowly and deeply, holding the air in your lungs for a count of three; then exhale just as slowly and deeply. Now relax your breathing, becoming more and more relaxed with each breath you take.

- And as you are relaxing more and more deeply, allow your thoughts to drift inward, imagine your thoughts focusing on the center of your awareness. Imagine or pretend your thoughts are going to the center of your awareness, and your thoughts will go there, simply and easily.

- Now imagine or pretend that there is a door in the center of your awareness. It can be any kind of door you choose. Take a moment to observe this door. Notice its size. Its shape. Notice if it has a color.

- This door opens to your zone. That place of perfect peace and clarity where you are fully, completely your best and highest self. You can open this door. You can choose to open it now. You can open this door and enter into your zone. Now gently and easily open this door. And step fully and completely into your best and highest self.

- Enjoy this experience of being in your best and highest self, allowing yourself to feel it as fully as you can at this moment. You own this space of perfect peace and clarity. It is yours.

- And as you are experiencing your best and highest self, hear the words, "This is my zone. This is my zone." You own this space of perfect peace and clarity.

- And any time you would like to return to your zone, any time you would like to touch in to this space, all you have to do is once again call up the image of your doorway. Call up the image of your doorway and say to yourself, "This is my zone," and you will return to this space of perfect peace and clarity.

- And now enjoy this space of perfect peace and clarity for a few moments more, and then take a deep, gentle, cleansing breath and come back to full awareness feeling alert and refreshed. Come all the way back, knowing that at any time you choose you can return to this space of perfect peace and clarity just by calling up your doorway and saying to yourself, "This is my zone."

As with any exercise, this one gets more results with repeated use. It isn't the only doorway to your zone by any means. It may not be one that works well for you.

The invitation to be playful, inventive in finding your zone, stands regardless of whether this one works for your or not.

Ours to find. Ours to enjoy.

About the Author

Maureen Smith writes about herself, "I had plans to be a normal person. I grew up in a middle class family with a brother and sisters and a dog and hamsters and a bird. I worked hard in school and got into college, where I started out on the normal route, choosing from column A: teacher rather than column B: nurse, and then moved right on from teaching kindergarten to being a full-time suburban wife and having babies. While I was doing the traditional mom thing, I took a part time job as an Avon lady, and found out that I could sell stuff. So I decided to upgrade, as they say in the computer industry, and worked my way into being a stockbroker and financial planner. But while I was working at being 'normal,' odd things kept happening. My parish priest observed that I 'saw too far.' My Avon customers started telling me their life stories. One of them bought from me just so I would listen to her poetry. Another asked me to light candles for her. I decided to get myself off to a good start at the beginning of my financial planning career by going to a workshop entitled 'Creating Money.' It turned out to be the first of spiritual growth seminars that I have been participating in for fourteen years now. As an investment advisor, I wound up with clients telling me about their life crises so often that I started to keep tissues on my desk. When one of them asked me if she could schedule another 'session' with me,

I decided I had to give up trying to be normal. I studied hypnotherapy and began offering my services without the cover of 'doing business.' And I wrote a newsletter. People loved it. I loved it. I wrote enough newsletters to turn them into a book, which isn't any more normal than I am."

That book was *Full Tilt Living*, her first. This book is *The ABCs of Full Tilt Living*, her second, which she wrote as a response to her clients' requests for ways to make changes in their lives and choices that would put them more in charge. She came up with playful ideas to share with them, and then more playful ideas appeared, and then there was a book. "*The ABCs of Full Tilt Living* is really twenty-six ways for me to show people I have cared for that I am still, and will always be, behind them all the way."

Maureen lives in San Francisco with her husband.